HAL•LEONARD
INSTRUMENTAL
PLAY-ALONG

HORN

T0055922

COLDPLAY

THE CD IS PLAYABLE ON ANY CD PLAYER, AND IS ALSO ENHANCED SO MAC AND PC USERS CAN ADJUST THE RECORDING TO ANY TEMPO WITHOUT CHANGING THE PITCH!

Cover photo: Peter Neill – ShootTheSound.com

ISBN: 978-1-4768-1836-8

HAL•LEONARD®
CORPORATION

7777 W. BLUEMOUND RD. P.O. BOX 13819 MILWAUKEE, WI 53213

Visit Hal Leonard Online at
www.halleonard.com

CONTENTS

CLOCKS

HORN

Words and Music by GUY BERRYMAN,
JON BUCKLAND, WILL CHAMPION
and CHRIS MARTIN

IN MY PLACE

HORN

Words and Music by GUY BERRYMAN,
JON BUCKLAND, WILL CHAMPION
and CHRIS MARTIN

EVERY TEARDROP IS A WATERFALL

5/6

HORN

Words and Music by GUY BERRYMAN,
JON BUCKLAND, WILL CHAMPION, CHRIS MARTIN,
PETER ALLEN, ADRIENNE ANDERSON and BRIAN ENO

FIX YOU

HORN

Words and Music by GUY BERRYMAN,
JON BUCKLAND, WILL CHAMPION
and CHRIS MARTIN

LOST!

9/10

HORN

Words and Music by GUY BERRYMAN,
JON BUCKLAND, WILL CHAMPION
and CHRIS MARTIN

small notes optional

PARADISE

HORN

Words and Music by GUY BERRYMAN,
JON BUCKLAND, WILL CHAMPION,
CHRIS MARTIN and BRIAN ENO

THE SCIENTIST

HORN

Words and Music by GUY BERRYMAN,
JON BUCKLAND, WILL CHAMPION
and CHRIS MARTIN

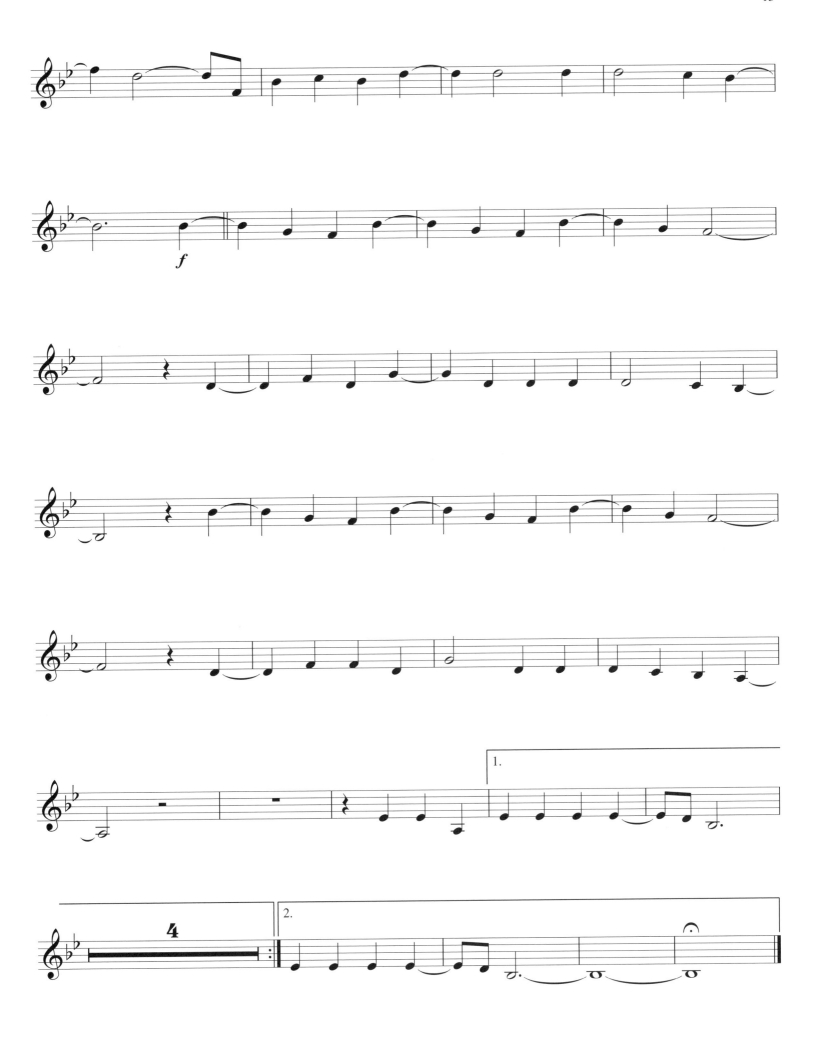

SPEED OF SOUND

HORN

Words and Music by GUY BERRYMAN,
JON BUCKLAND, WILL CHAMPION
and CHRIS MARTIN

TROUBLE

17/18

HORN

Words and Music by GUY BERRYMAN,
JON BUCKLAND, WILL CHAMPION
and CHRIS MARTIN

Moderately
Piano

VIOLET HILL

HORN

Words and Music by GUY BERRYMAN,
JON BUCKLAND, WILL CHAMPION
and CHRIS MARTIN

YELLOW

HORN

Words and Music by GUY BERRYMAN,
JON BUCKLAND, WILL CHAMPION
and CHRIS MARTIN

VIVA LA VIDA

 23/24

HORN

Words and Music by GUY BERRYMAN,
JON BUCKLAND, WILL CHAMPION
and CHRIS MARTIN